YOU CAN'T MAKE THIS #%*@ UP!

Laughable Simpleminded People

by H.O.

RoseDog Books

PITTSBURGH, PENNSYLVANIA 15238

RoseDog Books
585 Alpha Drive
Suite 103
Pittsburgh, PA 15238
Visit our website at *www.rosedogbookstore.com*

ISBN: 978-1-4809-7644-3
eISBN: 978-1-4809-7667-2

H.O.

H.O. was a former law enforcement investigator who worked in a large metropolitan city within the United States, with over thirty years in street investigations working in major crimes.

H.O. has worked assisting several State/Federal enforcement agencies over the course of his career.

Throughout his law enforcement career, H.O. has kept his sense of humor while dealing with the ugly side of human nature.

This book is dedicated to my family and friends who have supported my career in law enforcement.

H.O.

laugh-a-ble

Adjective

so ludicrous as to be amusing

Oxford Dictionaries

Simple-minded

Adjective

having or showing very little intelligence or judg-

ment

Oxford Dictionaries

Content

Chapter 1   New Police bicycle 1

Chapter 2   Wild cows 2

Chapter 3   Karma .3

Chapter 4   On Fire 4

Chapter 5   Stolen IPhone 6

Chapter 6   Naked man 7

Chapter 7   Minister's prize winning dog 8

Chapter 8   Officer down 9

Chapter 9   Skateboard 11

Chapter 10   Cruelty to animals 12

Chapter 11   Miniature poodle 14

Chapter 12   Captain' promotion 15

Chapter 13   Married co-workers 16

Chapter 14   Frozen body 17

Chapter 15   Saw off shotguns 18

Chapter 16   Police batons 19

Chapter 17   Merry Christmas 20

Chapter 18   Implants 21

Chapter 19   First day on the job 22

Chapter 20   Prostitute investigation 23

Chapter 21   Socks .24

Chapter 22   Stool sample 25

Chapter 23   Micro Manager 26

Chapter 24   Interrogation 27

Chapter 25   Prisoner's property 28

Chapter 26   1lb of marijuana 29

Chapter 27   Big Mac sandwich 30

Chapter 28   1.3 million 31

Chapter 29   Lieutenant's chair 33

Chapter 30   Lieutenant's new squad 34

Chapter 31   Guns drawn 35

Chapter 32   Nightgown 36

Chapter 33   Friend's name 37

Chapter 34   The phone call 38

Chapter 35   Oil change 39

Chapter 36   Drinking beer 40

Chapter 37   Sexual relations 41

Chapter 38   Attempted suicide 42

Chapter 39   Intoxication 43

Chapter 40   Alley behavior 44

Chapter 41   Domestic dispute 45

Chapter 42   Craigslist 46

Chapter 43   Last day 47

Chapter 44   Shrimping 48

Chapter 45   Dumpster diving 49

Chapter 46   Frying pans 50

Chapter 47   Expelled 51

Chapter 48   Russian's auto 52

Chapter 49   Taxi 54

Chapter 50   Basketball 56

Chapter 51   Detective's desk 57

Chapter 52   Baseball game 58

Chapter 53   Bro's night out 59

Chapter 54   Attempted Suicide 60

Chapter 55   Barking dog 61

Chapter 56   Medical Examiner 63

Chapter 57   Bowel Movement 65

Chapter 58   After hours 66

Chapter 59   Homicide suspect 67

Chapter 60   On duty sex 69

1. A Veteran officer, while riding his new police bicycle for the first time, sees his beautiful sister-in-law walking on the city street. As the veteran officer STARES at his sister-in-law, he collides with a parked auto, damaging the new police bicycle, the parked auto, and the veteran officer.

2. A community of new immigrant-Hmong citizens is acting suspicious in an alley next to a parked auto. Officers stopped and questioned the Hmong citizens regarding their suspicious activity. A search of the auto revealed inside then auto's trunk a large bloody animal cut into pieces. Officers believed the large animal could possibly be human body parts. Officers call in the medical examiner to assist in investigating the suspicious bloody body parts. The medical examiner advises the officers it most likely was a large animal and then leaves the scene.

Further investigation revealed the Hmong citizens were hunting for wild cows and found a heard of wild cows in a field, so they jumped a fence and killed a wild cow with butcher knives. They brought back the wild cow to share with their Hmong community. The Hmong community believed the cows were actually wild cows and not owned by farmers.

3.

An intoxicated man observes several police squads chasing an automobile in his neighborhood. He then observes one of the police squads hit an automobile at an intersection, causing severe damage and injuries to all the occupants in the automobiles. This intoxicated man decides to lie down next to the police squad and pretends to have been struck by the police squad. When other police arrive to the scene, police officers quickly realize no automobiles struck the intoxicated man. The police order the intoxicated man to leave the scene or be arrested for obstructing. The man leaves the area.

A short time later, the intoxicated man is struck by an automobile and severely injured by an intoxicated driver.

4. During many narcotic transactions, drug dealers often insist that the buyer smoke the narcotics with them. Drug dealers believe if the buyer smokes narcotics with them, the buyer cannot be an undercover officer.

A non-smoking undercover narcotic officer meets a drug dealer to conduct a drug transaction. The narcotic officer did not want to be asked to smoke marijuana by the drug dealer, so he smokes a cigar during this narcotic transaction. The undercover officer is attempting to purchase narcotics from this drug dealer for the first time. The drug dealer is suspicious of the undercover officer during this transaction. The undercover officer brings out a six-pack of beer to drink during the conversation to ease the suspicion by the drug dealer. As the undercover officer is smoking his cigar, drinking beer, and talking to the drug dealer, the officer's surveillance team observers the undercover officer's jacket start on fire, due to the cigar ash. Seconds later, the drug dealer tells the undercover officer he is on fire. The undercover officer puts out the flames and laughs with the drug dealer.

The drug dealer tells the undercover officer there is no way he is a police officer, so he sells the undercover officer a large amount of drugs.

5. A woman, Jenny, is having an affair with her husband's friend Bill. One day, after the two have sex, Bill steals Jenny's new iPhone and goes home. When Jenny's husband returns home, she tells him that his friend Bill stole her IPhone. Jenny and her husband go to Bill's home to retrieve her iPhone. Jenny and her husband force their way into Bill's apartment with a gun. During a struggle with persons inside the home, Jenny's husband shoots his friend Bill's roommate and the Jenny stabs Bill, who she has been having an affair with.

Jenny is arrested for reckless use of a weapon-knife and armed burglary. Her husband is arrested for reckless use of a weapon-gun and armed burglary.

The IPhone was recovered inside the apartment by police and seized as evidence for the criminal trail against Jenny and her husband.

6. Police get a tip for the location of a violent suspect wanted for a shooting. Officers go to the suspect's home during the night. As the police knock on the front door, the suspect observes the officers. The suspect gets naked and climbs to the roof of the house to avoid being seen and arrested. The police discover the suspect sitting on the roof' peak naked. The police order the naked suspect to climb down from the roof. The suspect refuses to come down, so the police call in the media.

Breaking news...naked man sitting on his roof to avoid being arrested, as the camera zooms in.

The police call the fire department and use the ladders to get the naked suspect down and to jail, all on live television.

7. A team of officers surrounds a home of a shooting suspect. One of the officers decides to wait in the neighbor's yard for a better view of the suspect's house in case the suspect flees the residence. The neighbor, an elderly man, sees the officer in his yard and orders the officer out of his yard. The officer advised the elderly neighbor he is a police officer, but the elderly neighbor does not hear the officer.

At this very moment, other officers enter the suspect's home. A detective orders the suspect's mother to put her poodle outside while they search for her son for the dog's safety. The mother puts her poodle outside in the yard.

Immediately, two gunshots are heard and the sound of a whimpering dog. The detective assumes fellow officers had shot this poodle he had just ordered outside.

As the detective goes outside to investigate the shooting, he discovered a fellow officer, while standing in the neighbor's yard, had shot this elderly neighbor's prize winning German Shepard, who's owner is a Minister of the cloth.

8.

A team of officers searches a home for a suspect. The suspect and his family are home. As officers clear the home of any danger, an experience tactical sergeant finds a small gun and puts it in one of the officer's inside jacket pocket. This experienced tactical sergeant tells the officer the gun is not loaded and safe.

Twenty minutes later, the sound of a gunshot is heard inside the home. Everyone in the home stops what they were doing while officers draw their weapons looking for a gunman. At this moment, an officer yells he has been shot. The suspect's father then has a seizure and falls to the kitchen floor. Officers advised the dispatcher an officer has been shot, so many officers and supervisors respond to the scene, including the police chief.

Officers tell the injured officer to get naked, so they can find the wound. So, the officer removes all of his clothing down to his underwear. Officers search the wounded naked officer's body for a bullet hole and observe a large contusion to the right side of his belly, but find no bullet hole. Many police officers and supervisors arrive at this time seeing the naked police officer not bleeding.

Detectives discovered the "unloaded" gun was loaded after all. As the officer had reached inside his jacket for a pen the gun went off accidentally striking the officer in an upward direction, striking his duty belt and lodging in the rim of the duty belt, causing a large contusion to his large belly.

9. A young beautiful women is walking to work early in the morning. A young man skate boarding approaches her. This young man stops in front of the women and raises his skateboard in a threatening manner and demands her money and cell phone. The women then kicks this young man in the groin and continues her walk as the young man is laying on the ground in pain.

The women called the police and the police arrest this young man for attempted armed robbery. This young man asks the officer if he can press assault charges on the women he tried to rob for kicking him in his groin.

10.

A women hired contractors for repairs to her garage. Being suspicious of the contractors, she installs a video monitor inside her garage to watch the contractors as they repair her garage. This woman is only able to view live video to her garage from inside her home. One day, she happens to look at her video monitor and observes her neighbor inside her garage. She assumes her neighbor is inspecting the contractor's recent work. She lets her one-year-old puppy out of her home to go play with the neighbor. While this woman is watching the video monitor, this neighbor sees the puppy and calls for the dog. As the neighbor and puppy begin to play, the puppy decides to lick the neighbor's groin area. This neighbor grabs the dog and decides to sexually assault the dog. This woman is shocked and appalled at her neighbor's behavior and calls 911. The women had to repeat her complaint to the police several times her neighbor is having sex with her dog in her garage.

The police arrive and find her neighbor and the puppy inside garage alone. The police advise this man the owner of the puppy had observed him having sex with her dog. The neighbor tells police he became sexually excited when the puppy licked him in his groin, so he decided to have sex with the puppy.

The neighbor is arrested for cruelty to animals.

11. A rookie officer is called to a complainant's home regarding her neighbor's dog barking excessively. As the rookie officer enters the complainant's home to investigate her neighbor's excessively barking dog, the complainant's miniature poodle approaches the rookie officer and barks at the rookie officer. The rookie officer shoots numerous times and kills the women's miniature poodle.

Training Order #1550

Train all 2,000 officers on the different breeds of dogs and their potential of violence as animals.

12. A police captain is heading to work for his night shift. On the way he stops and picks up a female prostitute. The police captain engages in a sexual act with the prostitute for money. During this sexual act, the police captain discovers the female prostitute is actually a man. The police captain orders the man out of his car, but the male prostitute demands money for his/her services before he leaves the car.

A struggle ensued and the police captain pulls out his service weapon. During the struggle, the police captain gun goes off and strikes the police captain in the face. The male prostitute then leaves the area.

The police captain then calls 911 and reports the following: he attempted to stop a robbery in progress against a female. He stopped the male suspect and a fight ensued, during the struggle the suspect grabbed his service revolver and shot him in the face.

The police captain stated he couldn't identify the suspect.

Months later, this police captain was promoted.

13.

James is a detective married to another detective on the police force. James attends a police conference at a hotel where he is seen with a fellow female police. James and the female police officer are not seen at the conference by his co-workers during the rest of the police conference. James's co-workers discovered that he and the female police officer had been sharing one room during the conference. When the conference is over James invites his detective wife to the hotel to spend the weekend alone.

Months later, James' wife, wo is also a detective, is investigating an assault complaint. The female victim notices the female police detective officer's last name and asks if she knows her boyfriend who has the same last name.

The female officer advises this victim her boyfriend is her husband. Soon to be ex-husband!

14. A long time police informant is arrested for several purse robberies. Detectives suspect the informant accidentally killed an elderly woman during one of the robberies, when she fell to the ground and hit her head. Detectives advise the informant he is in serious trouble, unless he provides information regarding other major robberies, shootings, or homicides incidents.

The Informant then tells officers about a frozen body in the lake. The informant related he, a friend, and the frozen victim were working at a local drug house. When the drug dealer left for dinner, he and his friend stole all the drugs from the house. When the drug dealer returned they accused the frozen victim of stealing the drugs. The drug dealers then kidnapped him and threw him in the lake to die. The informant provides a name of the victim.

The detective then calls the homicide unit and discovers they just discovered a frozen body in the lake and had the name given by the informant.

The informant is only given two years in prison for his crimes.

15. After a team of police officers raids a drug house during the day, officers call for a marked police wagon to convey several prisoners. The marked police wagon arrives and parks at the corner of an intersection. While several uniform officers are standing by the clearly marked police wagon an auto appears and two young men exit the auto, each holding saw off shotguns. Both young men fire their weapons at the recently raided drug house. Officers give chase and arrest the young men.

The young men are given probation and release from custody. Two years later, the same young men steal an auto. While driving the stolen auto, they lose control and kill four people walking on a sidewalk.

16. Several seasoned officers stop an auto for a traffic violation. The driver exits and flees on foot. Officers do not give chase of the driver. Officers then drive this auto to a vacant lot. Officers then use their police clubs to remodel the exterior body.

Unknown to the officers, a local neighbor- Block Watch Captain, witness the officers damaging the auto and filmed the auto being damage. This film was turned over to the media and the police department.

Later, the officers are suspended for one week without pay.

17.

An off duty intoxicated officer decides to steal a several Christmas trees from a Christmas tree lot. The officer takes the stolen Christmas trees and decorated several police squads with the Christmas trees. Several officers observed this intoxicated officer decorate the police squad, including the intoxicated officer's supervisor.

18. A female police sergeant is discussing her co-workers newly implanted breast implants in the common office where several officers were working. This female police sergeant then uses her two hands to feel the new implants.

Another female officer complains of this non-professional behavior to the police chief. The female police sergeant is given only a five-day suspension.

One year later, the female sergeant is promoted to lieutenant of police, then to Captain of Police and supervises the co-worker with the implanted breast implants.

19. A seasoned officer asks a rookie officer to see his new weapon on his first day on the street. The rookie officer hands the seasoned officer his gun. The seasoned officer discharges the gun in the air and hands back the gun to the rookie officer and advises the rookie officer his gun is working properly.

The rookie officer's next assignment was to check for the sounds of gunfire in his patrol area.

20.

A police sergeant and his team are ordered to arrest prostitutes in his district. The police sergeant has several young officers assist him in arresting prostitutes. The sergeant advises the young officers he would show then how to make an arrest of a prostitute. The sergeant picks up a prostitute on the street. The police sergeant and prostitute agree on a price for felicio. The prostitutes then complete the felicio act on the police sergeant. The prostitute is then arrested for prostitution. The police sergeant writes a report detailing the investigation and arrest and presents it to the district attorney's office for charging.

The case was dismissed, due to the police sergeant completing the sexual act with the prostitute.

The sergeant was given new training on investigating prostitutes and now is assigned desk duty.

21. During court testimony of a female being charged with prostitution the defense attorney complained of entrapment by the officer, because he was naked. The judge asks the officer, if, in fact, he was naked?

The officer replied, no your honor, I was wearing socks.

22. During a hotel prostitution sting a female undercover officer meets a prospective male in one room while her arrest team are in the next room. The undercover officer cannot get the prospective male suspect to state he wanted sex for money. The prospective suspect stated he only wanted the undercover officer to leave a sample of her stool on his chest. Quick thinking by the undercover officer she asks what he wanted to do with her stool sample. The suspect tells her he wanted to take it home then masturbate with it. Knowing this is sexual gratification she calls for the immediate arrest by her team. No one comes, due to the laughter of her co-workers.

23. A sergeant, known for micro-managing, decided to view his officers on the street without the officers' knowledge. One day the sergeant followed the offers to an assignment and hid in the bushes watching the officers at work. The officer quickly noticed someone in the bushes watching them so they drew their weapons towards the sergeant.

The micro-managing sergeant decided from then on to stay inside the office and manage his officers from a distance.

24. After a long day a detective interrogates a prisoner for a crime. Hours later the prisoner exits the interrogation room and approaches the detectives' office and politely advises the other detectives the interrogating detective fell asleep two hours ago and wanted to know when he can have his phone call.

25. After a man is arrested by officers for shooting a man he is interviewed at the scene by detectives. Another set of officers transported the suspect to the city jail to be processed. The jailer's first question to the prisoner is if he had any weapons or drugs on his person? The man hesitates and pulls out several bullets which later match the type used in the shooting. The man then states he has a loaded gun in his underwear that he used to shoot a man.

26. After bar closing an intoxicated man approaches a beat officer attempting to ask directions to his home. The officer immediately notices a pound of marijuana in a clear gallon plastic bag protruding from his front jacket pocket. The office asked the intoxicated man where he purchased the marijuana. The intoxicated man advises the officer he had just purchased a pound of marijuana at the tavern for a good price

27. Police are sent to a call for trouble with a man at a McDonald's drive thru at 4 pm. Officers arrive and discover a very intoxicated unconscious man in his car at the drive-thru window. The car was on and in gear. The man had his foot on the brake pedal and was holding a sandwich. The man had ordered a Big Mac and taken one bite of the sandwich then passed out at the drive thru window, blocking other drive thru customers. Officers could not awaken the intoxicated man before being arrested.

Days later, this same intoxicated man calls the police department and advises the officer he had misplace auto.

28.

A man has his laptop stolen from his residence. The next day, the man visits his sister at her residence. When the man enters his sister's home, she slaps him in the face. The man asks why she slapped him. The sister says for sending her sexual graphic pictures to her email account. This man explains to sister it had to be the thief who had stolen his laptop the other day. So, the man and his sister email the thief and hold several sexual conversations with the thief. The man's sister sends a picture of women in a sexy bikini to thief. The thief wants the sister to visit him to smoke some marijuana with him. The thief gives his home address to the sister. The man and sister call the police to report the stolen laptop and the address of the thief. The detective who took the complaint requests that his supervisor assign him to work on this investigation. The supervisor denies the request and orders the officer to give it to the patrol division. Realizing that this case was solvable, hthe detective asked a fellow female detective to investigate the complaint immediately. The female detective calls the man and sister and starts to investigate the case. The female detective pretending to be the sister emailed the thief and arranges a meeting at thief's house. The thief sends a naked picture of himself to the officer. The female detective and officers go to the thief's residence and find the stolen laptop and arrest the thief. The police search the laptop thief's house without a warrant and find 5 pounds of marijuana, 1 kilo of cocaine and $1,300,000.00 in cash. Police seized all the money and narcotics.

The thief is released without charges for releasing ownership of the $1,300,000.00 to the police department.

29. An aging police lieutenant asks a younger lieutenant to relieve him from the command desk for a few minutes. The younger lieutenant agrees and sits in the command chair, only to find out that the command chair was wet an had been soiled by the aging police lieutenant.

30.

An aging police lieutenant is parking his new squad in the lower garage. He proceeds to drive the squad down a parking ramp and forgets to turn, striking six police motorcycles.

The aging police lieutenant was ordered never to drive a police squad.

31.

A female police officer is having an affair with her supervisor, who is a married police lieutenant. Another, separate, married officer arrives to have an affair with the female officer and discovers his married police lieutenant supervisor in bed with her. Guns are drawn and threats are made to each other. The police are called to the house to investigate.

The responding officers realized all three co-workers work with them in the same district. No arrests are made, and no reports are filed. Both the married police lieutenant and married officer continue their affairs with the female officer for months.

32. A veteran officer volunteers to work a shift with a young female officer. Within the first hour the young female officer advised the veteran officer she has a new pink nightgown and he should she her in it, because her shrink advised her to get out more and have relationships.

After his shift, the veteran officer advises his supervisor never to assigned the young female officer with him again, because she nuts.

33.

Two police officers stop a suspicious man. The man uses his friend's name as his own. Officers check this name and discover a warrant for homicide for this person. Officers immediately draw their weapons and orders the suspicious man to the ground. Officer search this man and find marijuana in his pockets. The suspicious man tells the officer he lied about his name then gives his real name. Officer checks this name and discover no warrants for his arrest. Officer arrest the suspicious man for possession of marijuana.

34. Officers were sent to a death investigation and found a young person deceased in her home. Officers determined the dead person had been deceased for several hours. Officers looked for any suspicious evidence and found none. Detectives were called to further investigate the death, due to the young age of the victim. While detectives were there investigating, a neighbor asked the detective if the women in the house was ok, because he just received a phone call from the victim's cell phone, but did not hear her. Detective immediately asked the officers if they were playing with victims cell phone recently. One of the officers admitted she had been playing with the victim's cell phone and accidentally dialed the last numbered called.

35. A limited duty officer takes a police squad for an oil change at a private oil change facility. The officer is told to wait, due to a busy day. The officer decides he can not wait, so he grabs the police shotgun and points the weapon at the attendant and orders him to change the oil in the squad immediately.

The limited duty officer is later suspended for two days.

36. A police officer is at a homicide crime scene. The officer is told to collect evidence from the scene. The officer recovers an ice-cold bottle of Miller beer. The officer, knowing the department does not inventory liquid, drinks the beer and inventories an empty bottle of beer!

37. A police dispatcher cannot make contact with a police offer. The police dispatcher can hear an unintelligible communication coming from the officer's radio. Several officers are sent to locate this officer, fearing for the officer's safety. The officers find the missing officer at an ex-girlfriend's house in a compromising position...having sexual relations in the back seat of the squad while the police radio is ON!

38.

A senior officer is assigned a rookie officer to train. On the rookie officer's first tour of duty with the senior officer, they go to a house of prostitution. The senior officer orders the rookie officer to watch the police squad and do not answer the radio if called from the dispatcher. While the senior officer goes and collects on a personal debt from one of the prostitutes, the police dispatcher is attempting to send them to an emergency call for service. After 20 minutes, the rookie officer knocks on one of the bedroom inside the prostituting home. The senior officer exits the room partially undresses and yells at the rookie officer for interrupting his interrogation.

39.

One hot summer night, there is a police related shooting, where all the command staff is at the crime scene. A police patrol wagon is called to transport one of the suspects that had shot an officer. As the patrol wagon arrives, the patrol officer exits the patrol wagon and passes out next to the patrol wagon. As the police chief and command staff attempts to provide first aid, they discover the officer is highly intoxicated!

40.

Officers are patrolling a high crime area and notice a parked auto in an alley with two occupants. Officers approach the occupants and discover two men having sexual contact. One of the occupants identifies himself as the assistant police chief assigned to internal affairs. The assistant chief is arrested for lewd and mischievous behavior in a public street.

Within the hour, the police chief retires.

41. A women calls 911 and reports a domestic dispute with her husband who is currently home. Officer arrives and separates the couple. As one officer arrests the male, the other offer consoles the woman, at which time, the woman performs a sexual act on the officer in her residence, while the other officer waits outside with the husband.

42. A detective is going through a messy divorce with his wife. The detective decides to go on craigslist and find women for a sexual date. Weeks later, a woman he met through craigslist discovers she is pregnant and the baby is his!

This detective is happy and tells his co-workers he impregnated his craigslist date. The detective's co-workers check the women's name and discover she is a prostitute.

43.

A detective is set to retire after 27 years. This detective has worked in many violent, dangerous units within the police department.

On his last day, he is sent to investigate a shooting of a juvenile, who was shot three times. This detective identifies a suspect and requests the aide of witnesses to help capture the suspect. At the end of the detective's shift and last few minutes of his law enforcement career, he receives a call from the witness to the shooting. The witness tells the detective the location of the shooting suspect. Without hesitation, the detective goes to look for the suspect. The detective locates and arrests the suspect without incident. The suspect had in his possession the handgun used in the shooting and 50 bags of marijuana ready for street sale. After questioning the suspect, the suspect was attempting to kill his friend (victim), because he feared the victim would talk to the police regarding a homicide he had just committed.

Not bad for his last day on the police force.

44. A detective is investigating a reported rape. He arrives and meets a male victim. This male victim reports when he came home his boyfriend wanted to have sex. The male victim told his boyfriend he did not want to have sex at this moment. The boyfriend immediately grabs him and throws him on their bed and took off his pants. The boyfriend then began having anal sex with him. After injecting his sperm into the male victim, the boyfriend inserted a straw into his anus and sucked out all of his sperm. The male victim stated this was done without his consent. The detective asks the male victim if this sexual act had been done in the past with consent. The male stated several times and this act is call SHRIMPING, because you suck out the cocktail sauce.

No report was filed.

45.

A veteran officer is training a rookie officer. He tells the rookie they often eat out of garbage cans to save money in nice neighborhoods. Unknown to the rookie, the veteran officer had another officer put one half of a pizza in a box inside a garbage cart. So, the veteran office takes the rookie in an alley and opens a garbage cart. The veteran officer finds the pizza and shows the rookie. The veteran officer then offers part of the pizza. Still uncertain, the rookie declines to eat, however, the veteran officer eats the pizza. Days later, the rookie officer is with another officer and asks if they are to check the garbage carts for lunch, because he is low on cash.

46. A women has her boyfriend of two years arrested for beating her for the last two years. She tells the police she should have tied his ankles to the bedpost, poured some hot grits on him and burned him with the frying pans, because that's what mama said to do.

47. Several school officers escort three high school freshman girls out of the high school building without advising the school or their parents. The three girls do not go home; instead they go get massages and pedicures. After the massage and pedicures, they leave without paying for the services. The owner of the business pulls out his gun and chases girls. The owner shoots several times in the air while chasing the girls to stop them. The girl's stop and the owner of the business call the police. The same school officer's responds and arrest the business owner for shooting his weapon within the city limits.

All three girls were never arrested or cited.

48.

A women buys a $16,000 auto from an auto dealer with no credit and no money down. The women never makes a her monthly payment of $359.00 dollars. Two weeks later, these women total this auto in an accident. Two years later, a Russian body shop buys this auto as junk from the salvage yard. The Russian body shop restores the auto to its original quality. The Russian body shop advertises the auto for sale for $5,000. The original auto dealer sees the auto for sale and determines the auto is their auto they had sold several years ago to a women who never made a payment to them for the auto. The auto dealer wants car back and talk to the Russian body shop. The Russian body shop refused to return the auto to the auto dealer, because they purchased the auto from a salvage yard legally. The auto dealer hires a private investigator to find the women who had purchased the auto from them and has her report the auto stolen years ago before the auto was totaled in the accident. The auto dealer then calls the police and reports they have found their stolen auto. After the auto dealer and police harass the Russian body shop to return the stolen auto, they agree to give car back.

The Russian body shop strip the auto down to the frame, which is they way they had purchased the auto. The auto dealership refuses to repossess their auto and give it to the Russian body shop as gift.

49.

After having a wonderful date with his long time girlfriend, Ray went out in the middle of the night seeking a male for a sexual encounter. Ray used his father's work truck and found two males standing at a corner street and stopped and asked them if they needed a ride. The two males happened to be intoxicated and from out of town. The two males had called for a taxi and assumed this auto was the taxi, so they entered this auto.

During the ride Ray says he wanted to have the two males sexually assault him and he would pay them money. The two males agreed to assault the male for money. They stopped at a store and buy condoms and proceeded to Ray's father's work garage. Once in the garage Ray grabbed one of the male's genitals. The two males then battered and robbed him. The two males wanted more money, so he told them he had $1000 cash at his home. The two males then tied up Ray and put him in the trunk of his auto. As they drove to the Ray's house he told them he would give them the $1000 if they would have anal sex with him. Once there, the father sees his auto arriving and observed two strangers unload his tied up son out of the trunk of his auto. The father wakes up his other son and advises him to grab his gun, so he does. Two strangers opened the door and push the tied up boyfriend to the floor. Ray's brother shoots at the two strangers, striking one in the buttocks twice. The two men flee the area.

No one reports any of the crimes for an hour. After an hour, the father has Ray report a burglary to his work garage. The father advises everyone not to mention the shooting to the police. The police arrive and don't believe Ray's story, so they arrest him for reporting a false burglary complaint. Three hours later, one of the strangers arrives at a hospital with two bullet holes in his buttocks. This male tells the police he was shot by a stranger while walking for no reason. Detectives are called to investigate and discover the real story and everyone is arrested.

When Ray is arrested, he sends himself to a mental facility for treatment for his sexuality issues.

50.

On a hot summer day, an entire city block of teenagers play basketball in the middle of the street using a portable basketball hoop. During a break, the teenagers sit on a neighbor's porch. Three sisters who live in the home tell the teenagers to get off their porch and an argument occurs. The sisters warn the teenagers someone will come to take care of the matter. Phone calls are made by the sisters and 20 minutes later, the sister's stepbrother, with whom one of the sisters is having a sexual relationship, arrives with a gun. This stepbrother shoots at the crowd of teenagers and four teenagers are shot. The brother calmly walks away.

51. A detective is working at his desk. The detective is a hoarder and keeps his desk in an unkempt manner. A new lieutenant is assigned to this detective's unit and notices the detective's unkempt desk. The lieutenant does not like a unkempt work desk and orders the detective to keep his desk clean at all times. Well, other detectives hear this and throughout the week put numerous papers and food wrappings on the detective's desk. The lieutenant observes the detective's dirty desk and yells at the detective. An argument begins and the detective pulls out his service weapon and points his gun at the lieutenant. Many detectives step in and save the lieutenant's life.

This lieutenant now avoids this detective and his dirty desk.

52.

Several off duty detectives go to a baseball game with their supervisor in the middle of the day. This supervisor arranged a shuttle bus for everyone for the day. After the game, the supervisor insists they go to a gentleman's club. At the gentleman's club, the supervisor would not let the detectives spend any of their money. The supervisor bought everyone drinks while at the gentleman's club. At closing time, 2:00 am, the detective's notice their supervisor had left earlier with the shuttle bus. All the detectives were intoxicated and could not drive. All the men were afraid to call their wives for a ride, except one.

When this detective's wife arrived, several intoxicated men enter the auto and thank her by licking her hand and arm several times.

53.

Two best friends go out for the evening. After the evening is finished at about 2:00 am, Ed tells his friend Phil that he has to go home to his wife. Phil informs Ed that he is not going home, because it's guy's night out. Ed reiterates that he is going home. Phil then pulls out a gun and points it at Ed and tells him he is not going home. They park the car and continue the argument. Ed gets out of car and attempts to go home. Phil then pushes his friend and chokes him and tells him he is not going home, it is bro night out, and he will shoot the tires on his auto if he has to. Then he points the gun to Ed's head and again tells him he is not going home. Ed pushes the gun away and Phil shoots him in the hand, stating "Look what you made me do."

54.

Two comical police officers are sent to a suicide in progress. The suicidal subject is holding a large knife to his stomach and threatening to kill himself.

When the comical officers arrive, they observe the suicidal man holding the knife to his stomach and threatening to kill himself.

Immediately, one of the officers advises the suicidal man he should stab himself quickly before his partner shoots him in the head. The suicidal subject observes the other officer holding his handgun towards him and observes the officer's hands vigorously shaking. The officers again advise the suicideal man to stab himself quickly, advising him it is illegal to kill yourself, so this is why his partner has to shoot him in the head.

The suicidal man quickly drops the knife and the officers then seek mental help the suicidal man.

Weeks later, the two officers receive an award for saving this man's life.

55.

A young officer is sent to investigate a complaint of a loud barking dog.

As the officer interviews the complainant, he discovers the complainant is a sergeant in his police department. The sergeant stated that the neighbor's barking dog has annoyed his wife for several weeks. The owners leave the dog outside tied to a tree while they are at work. His wife attempted to talk to the neighbors, but was ignored by them. The sergeant said that over the past several weeks, this dog had been tied to a tree all day without water, while the owners are not home, according to his wife.

The officer then speaks to the neighbor who had the barking dog. The officer discovered the owners had just found their dog duct taped all over and tied to their tree when they returned home from work. The neighbors suspect the sergeant's wife of duct taping their little dog, because she constantly complains of their dog barking.

The young officer returns to the complaint's residence and attempted to speak to the sergeant's wife, but was not allowed by the sergeant. The young officer advised the sergeant that the neighbors suspect his wife of duct taping their dog to the tree.

The sergeant denies the allegations and orders the officer to leave his residence.

This investigation ended, due to lack of cooperation from the sergeant and his wife.

56. A four-week detective school for newly promoted city officers and six new federal postal inspectors was held in the police academy.

One day, the schedule included an afternoon four-hour class on armed robberies investigations. However, this day, the head medical examiner stopped in to give his four-hour class on homicides investigations. Due to the medical examiner's busy schedule, he was allowed to give his class after lunch.

As the medial examiner explains crime scene foren-sics and displayed graphic details of homicides, a loud noise came from the back of the classroom. As the new detectives look, they observe one of the new federal postal inspectors passed out on the floor.

The detective's instructor is then heard yelling at the head medical examiner "Doctor, Doctor, there is a man down back here".

The head medical examiner does not go toward the down passed out postal inspector, but instead, paces in the front of the room.

One of the detectives calls 911 an paramedics arrive and start to administer medical treatment to the past out postal inspector.

As the paramedics are treating the postal inspector, the head medical examiner approaches the paramedics and says" excuse me". The paramedics thinking the doctor is there to assist them move out of the way. The head medical examiner then steps over the postal inspector and grabs a cup of coffee and a doughnut.

Later, the detective's instructor advises the class the head medical examiner works on dead people and maybe was nervous to work on a live body.

57.

City drug narcotic officers and FBI agents arranged a narcotic meeting at a hotel with high-level narcotic dealers. The hotel room where the meeting is to take place (target room) is wired for sound and video. In the adjoining hotel room, all the narcotic officers and the FBI agents were waiting for the high-level narcotic dealers to arrive. In this restroom, agents had a 24" round high frequency digital sound recorder disk in the restroom pointed in the direction of the room where the narcotic meeting was to take place.

While waiting for the high-level narcotic dealers to arrive, a female FBI agent enters the target room and she enters the restroom. While in the restroom, the other agents hear the female agent on the audio recording unit having a bowel movement and see the female agent on the video camera.

58.

A company buys a used commercial building and refurbishes the building as a high quality indoor storage facility. The facility has a high tech security/video system in the facility.

One day, the owner notices on the security system, a certain unit was being used only during hours between 2:00 am and 5:00 am.

The owner opens the storage unit and discovers the unit was being used as living room/bedroom. The owner observed several beds, couches, and used condoms in the unit.

The owner asked the tenant of the unit what was occurring in the storage unit during hours between 2:00 am and 5:00 am. The tenant tells the owners, he has a side after hour business for an after hour "hook up" party for men on men.

The owner immediately evicted the tenant and raised rents.

59.

An over zealous, egotistical, arrogant, intelligent police supervisor leads a team of officers in making felony arrest.

One night, after working twelve hours and making numerous arrests, the supervisor advised his team he has a lead on a homicide suspect. Even though, the police team was exhausted, they agreed to go with the lieutenant to find the suspect at 2: 00 am.

Once at the front door of the suspect's residence, the officers knock on the door. An elderly woman opens the door and immediately the supervisor tells this woman her son was wanted for homicide. The elderly woman holds her chest and stumbles back to the couch. The elderly is now having trouble breathing. The elderly women's husband appears and asks the officers what had happen. The supervisor advised him his son had killed someone last night in the city. The man advises the supervisor that was impossible, because his son was on vacation in Mexico with his family. The supervisor then asks for his son's complete name. The husband gives his son's name.

The supervisor realizes they had the wrong house and person. The supervisor apologized to the couple and leaves the residence.

60.

A detective and his wife of ten years are having trouble conceiving a child. After numerous test and visits to the fertility doctor, the doctor advises to have sex between the hours of 1:00 pm and 5:00 pm when the wife ovulates. The detective working hours are between 4:00 pm and 12:00 am.

On the day the detective's wife is ovulating, the detective has to testify in court during the day before his shift. The detective spends the whole day in court. At 4:00pm, the detective finishes court and asks permission from the detective captain of police to go to his residence and have sex with his wife. The captain cannot believe his detective is asking permission to have sex with his wife on duty. The detective attempts to explain the fertility issues with his wife. The captain stops the detective and gives his consent to the detective.

The detective and his senior partner detective respond to the detective's residence using the red police lights and siren.

The detective calls his wife and advises her to be ready, because there are numerous shootings in the city and he has only a few minutes.

As the detectives arrive at the residence, the senior detective advises the detective if he needs any help with his wife, he is willing to use his lizard to get his wife pregnant.

The End

CPSIA information can be obtained
at www.ICGtesting.com
Printed in the USA
LVOW13*2150280817

546663LV00013B/297/P